CW01666372

More PO… PUB WALKS
Cheshire

David H. Pill

COUNTRYSIDE BOOKS
NEWBURY BERKSHIRE

First published 2013

COUNTRYSIDE BOOKS
3 Catherine Road
Newbury, Berkshire

To view our complete range of books, please visit us at
www.countrysidebooks.co.uk

ISBN 978 1 84674 285 9

For Michael and Wendy Rayner, good friends and good companions

Photographs by the author

Designed by Peter Davies, Nautilus Design
Produced through MRM Associates Ltd., Reading
Typeset by CJWT Solutions, St Helens
Printed by Berforts Information Press, Oxford

Contents

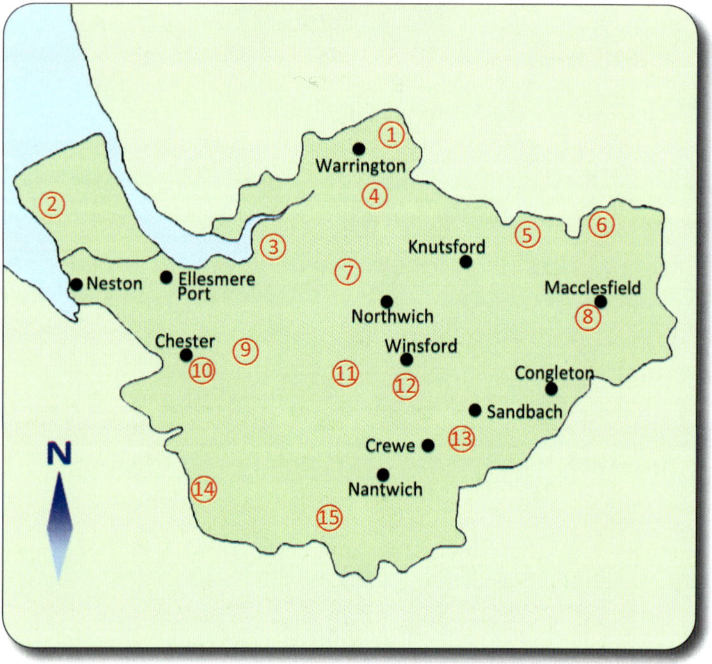

Area map showing location of the walks

Introduction

The walks in this book are intended to be enjoyed by all the family and the family dog (but please keep it on its lead when there are farm animals about). You will walk along a Roman road, a drover's road, a packhorse track and several canal towpaths, as well as field paths and leafy lanes. These will take you to some of Cheshire's loveliest villages, with their village greens, thatched cottages and ancient churches, as well as to some of the black and white, timbered manor houses for which the county is famous. You will also stroll through forest and woodland and alongside river and lake, and see castles, a medieval priory and an early cotton mill.

Most of the walks are on the Cheshire Plain and there is only one longish, steep climb (on the Wirral), but from several there are views of the hills. Do remember, by the way, to stop from time to time and look behind you or you are going to miss some beautiful scenery. Take time to observe the flora and fauna too. It is always worthwhile taking binoculars with you, not just for bird-watching but because some stiles and gates are hard to spot. And please be aware that stiles are gradually being replaced with gates throughout the county. There will be the occasional muddy patch too, so do make sure you are well-shod, preferably with boots. You should encounter few difficulties, however, and I suggest ways of avoiding the worst.

Each walk begins at a pub, except for two routes where they are about a mile distant, and descriptions and contact details are provided. There are also children's playgrounds on some of the walks, and most of the recommended places to visit should appeal to younger members of the family.

There is nothing like a good walk in good company, and I wish to thank my companions Roy Killcross, Peter Mather, Michael, Wendy, Alison and Freya Rayner, and Elaine Sims for their support and encouragement.

Happy walking!

David Pill

Publisher's Note

We hope that you obtain considerable enjoyment from this book; great care has been taken in its preparation. However, changes of landlord and actual closures are sadly not uncommon. Likewise, although at the time of publication all routes followed public rights of way or permitted paths, diversion orders can be made and permissions withdrawn.

We cannot, of course, be held responsible for such diversion orders and any inaccuracies in the text which result from these or any other changes to the routes nor any damage which might result from walkers trespassing on private property. We are anxious though that all details covering the walks are kept up to date and would therefore welcome information from readers which would be relevant to future editions.

The simple sketch maps that accompany the walks in this book are based on notes made by the author whilst checking out the routes on the ground. They are designed to show you how to reach the start, to point out the main features of the overall circuit and they contain a progression of numbers that relate to the paragraphs of the text.

However, for the benefit of a proper map, we do recommend that you purchase the relevant Ordnance Survey sheet covering your walk. The Ordnance Survey maps are widely available, especially through booksellers and local newsagents.

1 Glazebury

The Foresters Arms

Glazebury, once in Lancashire, has since 1974 been Cheshire's most northerly village. The River Glaze is the county boundary and we cross it to enjoy Windy Bank Wood, a mixture of ancient woodland and new planting which is part of Greater Manchester's Red Rose Forest. We then walk through sheep pasture to see two remarkable old houses. Having crossed the historic Liverpool to Manchester railway, the world's first inter-city line, we skirt the Carrs – farmland which was once moss – to pass between paddocks back to our pub.

Distance – 4½ miles.

OS map Explorer 276 Bolton, Wigan and Warrington (GR: SJ670980)

Starting point The Foresters Arms, Glazebury. Walkers may use the pub's car park but do ask permission first.

How to get there *The Foresters Arms, Glazebury, is on the A574 Warrington to Leigh road, just south of its junction with the A580.*

Level easy walking along farm tracks and woodland and field paths. A delightful walk suitable for all ages.

THE PUB

The **Foresters Arms**, a tiny place dating from the 1630s, has a forester with an axe on its weather vane. A friendly community pub, it is popular with walkers, who, if they give notice of their arrival, may get a meal outside normal hours. There are special rates for groups of two or more and the menu includes lamb Henry, rib eye steak, salmon in a peppercorn sauce, home-made pies and several different curries, plus a Sunday roast. Tetley's, Boddington's and John Smith's beers are available and there is always a guest ale on draught.

Open from 12 noon to 3.30 pm and 7 pm to 12 midnight Monday to Friday, and 12 noon to 12 midnight Saturday and Sunday. Food is served from 12 noon to 3.30 pm Monday to Friday; 12 noon to 9 pm Saturday; and 12 noon to 7 pm Sunday. ☎ 01942 673418; postcode WA3 5LG.

1 From the Foresters Arms, cross the road with care and turn left and then right onto a quiet lane. Ignore the footpath sign on the right and cross the River Glaze. At the T-junction, turn right to walk between the river and pasture.

2 Take the first track on the left to pass a picnic table on the right and walk into the new plantations of Red Rose Forest. Continue under the shade of more mature woodland into a wetland area where, in summer, you may see several varieties of butterfly, as well as damson and dragonflies seeking midges. At a tree-shaded junction, go left and then right and then, after a stretch of open ground, ahead at a further junction to enter a wood of birch and rowan. On emerging from it opposite Windy Bank Farm, turn left onto a broader track.

The River Glaze

3 Where the track swings to the right, take a path on the left. Go left at a junction and cross a stile into a meadow. Turn half left and follow a well-worn path towards the railway. On reaching it, turn right and then left to pass under the line. Where the way becomes wider and paved, look towards the right for the beautiful Light Oaks Hall, a remnant of a once larger 17th-century house. Where the track bends to the left, take the stile ahead into a field and look for another stile on the right. Cross the meadow to a metal gate and a footbridge over the river to emerge onto the main road.

4 If you require refreshment at what is virtually the halfway point of the walk, turn right to the George and Dragon. Otherwise, cross the road to a footpath sign. Go along the field track to its end and then bear right. Go ahead at the direction post and, on reaching the railway, turn left to pass through a gate on the right. This is a busy line. Cross it with care.

5 Go along a short narrow path which has good views to the right towards Glazebury church. Turn right at its end. Do take a closer look at the wood store on the left. Dating from the 14th century, it was the great hall of an otherwise vanished house, Hurst Hall. Keeping it on your left, go ahead through the farm gateway and turn left. There are now excellent views towards Winter Hill in the Lancashire Pennines. Cross a footbridge over the Carr Brook and then go right and left to walk along the right-hand edge of a field.

6 Having crossed a farm track, look for a stile on the right. Walk along the right-hand edge of the field. At its end, turn right onto a stony track. Follow this between paddocks to eventually turn left at a T-junction. There may be guinea fowl in your path as you approach Wards End Farm, where you should turn right. Look out for the various waterfowl around the pond to your left as you return to the Foresters Arms.

Place of interest nearby

Kenyon Hall Farm, 4½ miles west of the Foresters Arms, has plenty to entertain the children, including a big adventure play area and, in late summer, a maize maze. Adults have the opportunity to pick their own fruit and vegetables or visit the café or farm shop, where the local produce includes the farm's award-winning jams and chutneys. ☎ 01925 765531; postcode WA3 7ED

2 Thurstaston

The Cottage Loaf

This walk starts in Thurstaston but is really an excursion through the woods and fields which surround the Wirral village of Irby. First we pass through paddock and meadow to 17th-century Irby Hall. Then we walk through National Trust-owned Harrock Wood to Arrowe Park, Wirral's largest public park. After a stop for refreshment at the picturesque Irby Mill Inn, we pass through more National Trust woodland to climb Thurstaston Hill for splendid views of the Dee estuary and the Irish Sea, and across the Wirral peninsula to Liverpool.

Distance – 5 miles.

OS map Explorer 266 Wirral & Chester; GR: SJ247846.

Starting point The Cottage Loaf pub at Thurstaston. Patrons may leave their cars in the pub car park while they walk but please seek permission first. Otherwise, use the public car park just to the north of the pub.

How to get there *The Cottage Loaf is on the right of the A540 Chester to Hoylake road about 2¼ miles north-west of Heswall town centre.*

Apart from an optional climb at the end, this is easy walking over gently undulating ground.

THE PUB

The **Cottage Loaf** has catered for generations of walkers, from the 1920s as a tea room and from the 1950s as a pub. A Greene King house, it has its own special brew, Cottage Quencher. On the menu are award-winning fish and chips, beef and Ruddle's ale pie, lemon and thyme-glazed chicken breast and, on Sunday, slow-cooked lamb shank. Roasted sweet potato, broccoli and red onion tatin, roasted butternut squash risotto with wilted baby spinach, and peppered mushroom suet pudding are amongst the vegetarian dishes. Desserts include mascarpone and Madagascan vanilla cheesecake, Eton mess and, (welcome after walking in cold weather) a trio of mini hot puddings, with custard. And, by the way, 'kids eat free'.

Open from 11 am to 11 pm every day. Food is served from 12 noon to 10 pm. ☎ *0151 648 2837; postcode CH61 0HJ.*

1 From the Cottage Loaf, turn left and at the roundabout cross Thurstaston Road to enter a footpath signposted to Irby. Go through a kissing gate and along the drive of a barn conversion. Pass through a farm gate and walk along a track to a stile. Cross it and turn right to walk along a well-worn path, passing a duck pond on your right. Cross a further stile and follow a narrow path between a paddock and some houses, turning left onto a wider track. At its end, turn right to pick up another path at the end of a short cul-de-sac. Bear left and walk up the meadow to emerge via a kissing gate into Irby village.

2 Turn right to pass Irby Hall. See if you can spot the moat which defended an earlier house. Carefully cross the road and turn left into Woodlands Road. At its end, fork left and cross a stile to walk

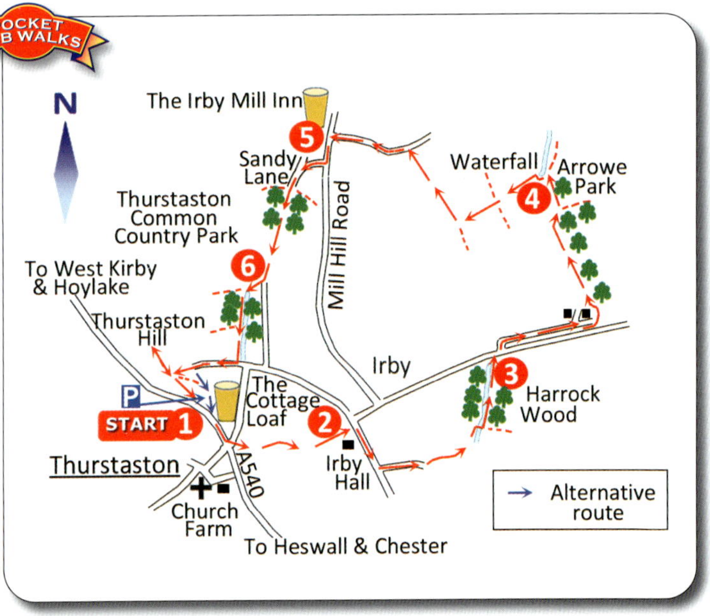

The start of the walk

along the right-hand edge of two meadows. Go through a gate, cross a stream and pass through another gate. Turn left to walk through Harrock Wood.

3 Cross the road ahead with care and turn right to walk along a quieter parallel road. After the white houses, return briefly to the main road. Turn left into a public footpath and left again to cross a wooden bridge into Arrowe Park. Bear right and follow the main path to its end, and then turn right and left into a tree-lined avenue. Where this begins to bend to the right, go left along a narrower path, passing a waterfall on your right. Cross a bridge and bear left to a kissing gate.

4 Bear right and then left to walk along the right-hand edge of several fields. Having crossed one track, turn right into a second

and walk to its end. Turn left onto a road and walk along its verge.

5 At the Irby Mill Inn, once a windmill's grain store, turn left into Mill Hill Road and right into Sandy Lane. Bear left as you approach a bungalow and keep ahead at the next bend to enter a bridleway. Follow this until it becomes a metalled road.

6 Now turn right to enter Thurstaston Common Country Park. Having crossed a stream bed, turn left and continue ahead, ignoring all paths to the right, until you emerge onto a road. Turn right onto School Lane. At its end, you may, if you are tired, turn sharp left to return to the Cottage Loaf. Otherwise, go diagonally left to climb Thurstaston Hill and, at the top, walk to a bench to your right to enjoy the view. Now retrace your steps briefly, but after the triangulation point look for a downhill path on the right. This will take you to the public car park. To reach the pub, bear left onto a path parallel to the road and pass a picnic table on your left.

Place of interest nearby

Church Farm, overlooking the River Dee, less than ¼ mile from the Cottage Loaf, has a café and farm shop, a crazy golf course, a pedal go-kart track and an adventure playground. It also has lots of animals, including meerkats, alpacas, donkeys, rabbits, guinea pigs and pygmy goats, some of which children may feed and cuddle. ☎ 0151 648 7838; postcode CH61 0HW.

More POCKET PUB WALKS

3 Norton

Evenwood Farm

Norton village has been swallowed up by Runcorn New Town but it still has some delightful rural aspects and a special treasure – the remains of a 12th-century Augustinian priory. From the priory, we walk through the parkland of the now vanished mansion which succeeded it. This is now two public parks, Phoenix Park and Town Park, where, in addition to the house's ornamental lake and still recognizable 18th-century landscaping, there are wild flower meadows, children's play areas and, operating at weekends, a miniature railway. A landmark on the walk is Norton Tower, a water tower built in 1890 as part of a scheme to supply

Distance – 4¾ miles.

OS map Explorer 275 Liverpool, St Helens, Widnes and Runcorn; GR SJ548832 (start of walk); GR SJ563838 (pub).

Starting point Norton Priory car park, or, if closed, park nearby on Tudor Road.

How to get there *Norton Priory (WA7 1SX) is signposted from the A558, about 1¾ miles west of its junction with the A56 Warrington-Chester road at Daresbury.*

Four short flights of steps, but generally level, easy walking.

Liverpool with water from Lake Vyrnwy in mid Wales. From it we return to the priory along the towpath of the Bridgewater Canal, opened in 1776 to link Liverpool with Manchester.

THE PUB

Evenwood Farm is built on farmland at the edge of a wood but it is not a former farmhouse. It is a very comfortable, modern pub, approximately a mile east of Norton Priory. The chef's pride is his carvery, but the pub also serves breakfasts and alternative main courses, which include beef in Chianti, hearty lamb and vegetable pie, smoked haddock Florentine and smothered chicken. There is also a wide variety of vegetarian dishes, plus hot and cold sandwiches, and an enormous choice of puddings. John Smith's beers are always available, and there are usually at least two guest beers, Old Speckled Hen being a frequent visitor.

Open from 10 am to 11 pm Monday to Saturday, and 11.30 am to 10.30 pm Sunday. Breakfast is served from 10 am to 11.30 am; the main menu from 12 noon to 9 pm. ☎ 01928 571328; postcode WA7 1SH.

1 Take the footpath to the right of Norton Priory's gate, signposted to the Bridgewater Way. On reaching the canal, go over the bridge, left, down the steps and left again.

The Bridgewater Way is a 39-mile long walk on the towpath of the Bridgewater Canal from Leigh in Greater Manchester to Runcorn, including a 3-mile spur into the centre of Manchester.

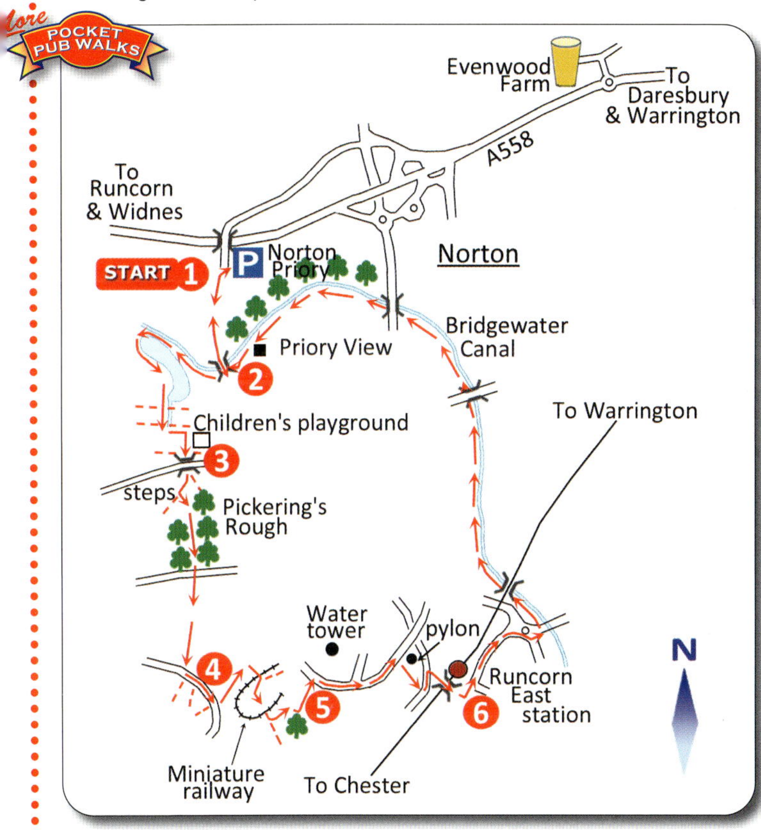

The remains of Norton Priory

2 Walk along the towpath to just before a modern road bridge. Here, turn left and follow a path along the right bank of the lake. When it turns away from the lake, continue along it, keeping a sometimes dry watercourse on your left. At a T-junction, continue ahead on the grass to cross another path. Turn left onto the next path, cross a bridge and turn right to walk alongside a children's playground.

3 Go ahead at a cross path, keeping a picnic table to your left. Pass under a road bridge to enter a wooded dell, Pickering's Rough. Ignore the steps immediately on the left and go ahead to cross a bridge to some further steps. At the top of the first flight, turn left. Cross a lane, continue ahead through a more open area and turn left onto another lane.

4 After passing the second of two short paths into a housing estate,

take a left fork. Go right at a junction of paths to cross the miniature railway and right again at the picnic tables. Pass a pond on your left and after crossing the railway track again, go immediately left onto a mown path. Pass to the left of a clump of trees and head towards the right of Norton water tower to eventually reach a lane.

5 Turn right and, on reaching a pylon, right again onto a footpath. At its end, turn left and cross the road. Go down the steps to the right of the bus shelter and cross a railway footbridge.

6 Turn left onto a lane, taking care when the pavement ends. Go ahead at the roundabout and turn left onto a canalside path. Ignore all the bridges until you have passed Canal Reach and the colourful Priory View mural. Ascend the steps at the next bridge and turn right to return to the priory.

Place of interest nearby

Norton Priory is one of the largest excavated monastic sites in Europe. Home to Britain's biggest medieval statue, its grounds include a medieval herb garden, an award-winning walled garden and a learning garden and play area. ☎ 01928 569895.

4 Appleton Thorn

The Thorn Inn

There has been a thorn tree at Appleton Thorn since the time of the Crusades. From it we cross fields to the village of Stretton, where we walk part of King Street, the Roman road which linked the salt mines of mid-Cheshire with the industrial settlement at what is now Warrington. We then drop down into the Mersey valley, passing through a dramatic sandstone cutting to join the Bridgewater canal at Stockton Heath. Finally, we walk up the wooded Lumb Brook valley and along a tree-shaded lane back to Appleton Thorn.

Distance – 6¾ miles.

OS map Explorer 276 Bolton, Wigan & Warrington (GR SJ637838).

Starting point The Thorn Inn, Appleton Thorn. Patrons may use the pub's car park whilst they walk, but please seek permission first. Otherwise, park by the green close to the inn.

How to get there *Appleton Thorn is on the B5356 about 1½ miles east of its junction with the A49 at Stretton and a similar distance south-west of junction 20 on the M6.*

One short, steep, downhill path, but otherwise level, easy walking punctuated by a gradual descent into the Mersey valley and a gentle climb back.

THE PUB

The **Thorn Inn**, with its panelled walls and shelves of old books, has something of the air of a gentlemen's club. Part of the Chef and Brewer chain, the pub's interesting menu includes venison and herb pie, wild boar burger with mulled plum chutney, chicken en croute, a seafood mixed grill and Mediterranean vegetable tart. Eton mess cheesecake and raspberry brownie torte are amongst the desserts. Black Sheep, Wells' Bombardier and IPA are always on draught and there is usually at least one guest beer.

Open from 12 noon to 11 pm Sunday to Thursday, and 12 noon to 12 midnight Friday and Saturday. Food is served from 12 noon to 10 pm Monday to Saturday, and 12 noon to 9.30 pm on Sunday. ☎ *01925 264362; postcode WA4 4QX.*

1 From the pub car park, cross the road to read the plaque about the history of the thorn tree. Now take the lane to the left of the war memorial. Turn left onto a footpath signposted to Blackcap Road. At its end, cross the road and walk along the left-hand edge of a field. Turn right into the next road and eventually left onto a path. Walk along the left-hand edge of several fields before entering a bigger, open field. Walk to the post ahead and turn left. At the road, turn right and walk to Stretton church.

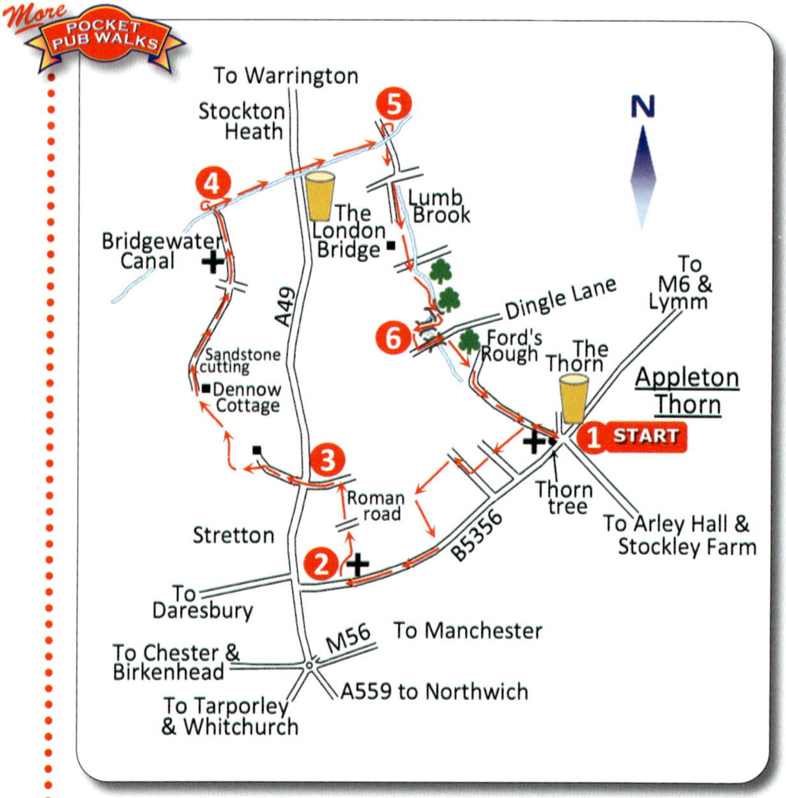

On the old Roman road

2 Just after the church, turn right onto a footpath which follows the route of the Roman King Street. (The name 'Stretton' means 'the place on the Roman road'.) Go straight ahead at the parish map to eventually cross one road and turn left onto another by a Janus-headed column.

3 Cross the A49 into Hillside Road. Where the road becomes a drive, cross a stile on the left onto a metalled path. Cross another and walk along the left-hand edge of a field. Continue ahead up a lane, passing Dennow Cottage on your right and a small green on your left. The obelisk is said to mark the burial place of Oliver Cromwell's horse. Go uphill to pass through a sandstone cutting. At the junction the road becomes busier and there is no pavement, so go into Hillcliffe chapel yard and walk along its right-hand edge. Continue along the road until you have crossed the canal bridge.

4 Turn left and left again onto the towpath. If you wish to call at the London Bridge pub, leave the canal at Thorn Marine chandlery. Otherwise continue along the towpath. The steps on the right after the bridge were once used by passengers on canal packet boats. Do not leave the towpath by the permissive path, but carry on until you have passed over a road. Here take the steep, narrow path on your left.

5 Turn left, go under the canal, cross the brook on your right and walk past the houses. Cross the road and walk up Dale Lane to take a footpath signposted to Dingle Lane which passes to the left of a school playing field. Carry on ahead, following the Lumb Brook all the way.

6 On reaching a lane, turn left, cross a bridge and turn right into the wood called Ford's Rough. At the end of the woodland path, turn right and left into Green Lane, which will take you back to Appleton Thorn.

Place of interest nearby

Four miles from the Thorn pub, **Stockley Farm** is a working farm where visitors can watch the cows being milked and also feed the lambs and goats. There are play and picnic areas, a pets' corner, a miniature golf course and a tea room. ☎ 01565 777323; postcode CW9 6LZ.

More POCKET PUB WALKS

5 Styal

The Ship

Styal is a picturesque village, where 18th-century mill workers' houses are interspersed with lovely thatched and timbered cottages. Our walk takes us through meadowland to Lindow Common, a rare relic of the heathland which once covered this part of Cheshire. We pass alongside a lake and over the wide expanse of Pownall Park to Wilmslow's impressive late medieval church. There we enter The Carrs, perhaps the most beautiful part of the valley of the River Bollin. We then follow the river through woodland back to Styal. And, in the shape of a distorted figure-of-eight, it can easily be shortened or done as two separate walks.

Distance – 6 miles, or two walks of approximately 3 miles each.

OS map Explorer 268 Wilmslow, Macclesfield and Congleton (GR: SJ839834).

Starting point The Ship Inn, Styal village. Patrons may leave their cars while they walk but please ask permission. Otherwise park carefully on the village street.

How to get there *The Ship is reached by turning left off the B5166 Wilmslow to Sale road, into Altrincham Road, 1¾ miles north-west of Wilmslow town centre.*

A few gentle slopes to negotiate but, on the whole, level, easy walking.

THE PUB

The **Ship** is a 300-year-old village inn, with 200-year-old wisteria growing up its walls. Popular with walking clubs, it serves Wells' Bombardier, and Theakston's Old Peculier is a regular guest bitter. The varied menu changes with the seasons. On it you may find beef and ale pie, rump steak in a garlic mushroom sauce, chicken in tomato and basil sauce and vegetable burritos, as well as various salads. The pub also does a hearty all-day breakfast and impressive combo meals, including an Indian platter for two.

Open from 12 noon to 11 pm every day. Food is served from 12 noon to 8 pm (9 pm on Tuesdays and Thursdays) ☎ 01625 523818; postcode SK9 4JE.

1 From the Ship Inn car park, turn left then right into the main road and right again into Holts Lane. At the junction, go ahead onto a path past the Apprentice House, where orphan apprentices at Quarry Bank Mill were boarded. You may visit its kitchen garden free of charge before crossing the road ahead onto a path along the right-hand side of a car park.

2 At the car park's far end, go through two kissing gates and walk along the right-hand edge of a field onto a fenced path. Here look out for old English longhorn cattle grazing to your left. Continue

along a downhill section paved with setts, testimony to its past as a pack-horse track. Do not follow the path as it swings to the right, but continue ahead across the meadow. Go through a gate and turn right. If you wish to halve the length of your walk, turn right again onto a riverside path (point 7). Otherwise, carry on ahead, crossing a tributary of the River Bollin to another car park.

The path through The Carrs

3 Bear right to cross the river itself, then go straight ahead along a broad tree-lined path. Go uphill and then left into the rough-surfaced Carrwood Road. Immediately take a narrow path on the right between fences. On reaching a made-up road, go ahead to pass the gates to Pownall Hall, once the home of the Boddington brewing family, and walk alongside Pownall Hall Farm. At the next road, turn right and then left.

4 Cross the main road with care onto an unmade road. Continue briefly on the metalled road ahead, then turn left into a wooded footpath onto Lindow Common. Go over the first cross-path and turn left at the second to briefly follow a broad path along the left bank of Black Lake. At a junction of paths, go left and immediately right onto a narrow path to emerge onto a road.

5 Turn left and right onto the main road. Cross at the pedestrian crossing and turn left and right into Pownall Park playing fields. Cross them to the trees on the far side and turn right onto a tarmac path. At a fork, bear left to walk between garden fences. Turn right

into Hawthorn Lane and walk to its end. Here, if you require refreshment, walk across the junction to the Bollin Fee pub. Otherwise, turn left.

6 Walk through Wilmslow churchyard, keeping to the left of the church tower. Turn left onto a lane and, having passed the children's playground and parish hall, turn left again onto a public footpath. Keep left to join a broader track through The Carrs. Cross the bridge over the Bollin and turn right. Ignore a second bridge and cross the third to return to point 3 and briefly retrace your earlier steps until you come to a gate on the left.

7 Go through the gate and follow the river, ignoring all paths to the left. Cross the wooden Herons Pool Bridge to pass a mill dam and a children's playground and arrive at Quarry Bank Mill.

8 Walk uphill past the mill and another play area. Take the path on the left signposted to Styal village. Walk through a field, cross a lane and walk ahead to a gate by the village cross. Turn right and, at a bench, bear right. At the Methodist church, turn left onto a cobbled lane. At its end, turn right to pass a tea garden and return to the Ship Inn.

Place of interest nearby

Quarry Bank Mill (National Trust) is an excellent example of an early cotton mill, with working machinery. Admission includes a visit to the Apprentice House. ☎ 01625 527468; postcode SK9 4LA.

6 Poynton

The Farmers Arms

Poynton, at the foot of the Pennines, was once a mining village; now it is a smart commuter town. Our walk links the park and lake of a vanished great house, Poynton Hall, with the park of a surviving one, Bramall Hall. We walk from the lake, Poynton Pool, alongside field and paddock and the golf courses of leafy Bramhall. (In case you are puzzled, the village is spelled Bramhall, the hall Bramall.) After skirting a wooded ravine, we pass the elaborate 16th-century front of the hall. Then we walk alongside the Lady Brook into the delightful and well-named Happy

Distance – 6½ miles.

OS map Explorer 268 Wilmslow, Macclesfield & Congleton (GR: SJ923848).

Starting point Car park in Anglesey Drive, Poynton.

How to get there *Anglesey Drive, SK12 1BT, is on the right of the A523 Macclesfield to Hazel Grove road, a mile north of Poynton town centre.*

Although one of the longer walks in the book, it is easy walking.

Valley, returning to Poynton by way of pasture and woodland, and enjoying good views of the Pennines.

The **Farmers Arms** is situated in Park Lane, Poynton, a mile south of the start of the walk. It was once a small beer house for miners. Today the extended pub is very much at the heart of the community. It is particularly popular on Sundays, when a traditional roast is served. There is a varied weekday menu, but the chef is especially proud of his pies of the day, which include steak and onion, steak and kidney, cheese and onion, minted lamb and ham and leek, all served with excellent home-made chips. The pub is a Robinson's house and its beers include Unicorn, Double Hop IPA and a special seasonal brew.

Open from 11 am to 11 pm Monday to Friday and 11 am to 1 am Saturday and Sunday. Food is served from 12 noon to 3 pm Monday to Friday and 11 am to 5 pm Saturday and Sunday. ☎ 01625 875806; postcode SK12 1RE.

1 From the car park, walk south along a narrow path, keeping Poynton Pool to your left. On reaching a bench, take the short path to your right and cross the main road onto the pavement of Glastonbury Drive. Where this road bends to the right, cross it to enter first a narrow path and then a bridleway. Ignore the road to the farmhouse on the right and the footpath to the left and carry on along the track ahead. Go through the gate at Lower Park Lodge and, ignoring paths to the right, walk on to a junction with a busy road. Turn left and cross the bridge with care.

2 Just after the white house on the right at the junction, look for a footpath sign in a hawthorn hedge. Walk to the right of the electricity substation and along the right-hand edge of a field. Cross a concrete road and a stile. Find another stile on the right and walk

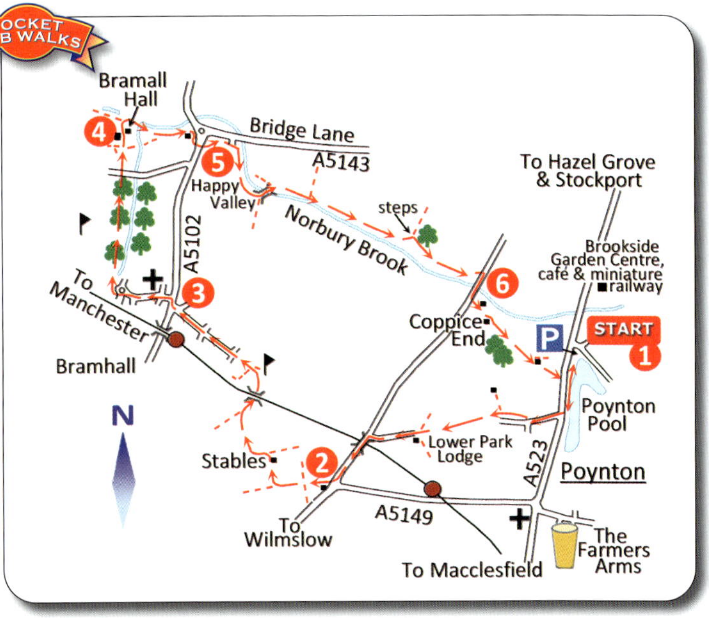

Historic Bramall Hall

under the trees and past the stables to a further stile. Turn left and follow the metal fence round to the right. Bear right at the Fred Perry Way sign, go under the railway and eventually right again to cross a wooden bridge. Turn left at the golf club entrance and walk along Ladythorn Road to its end.

The Fred Perry Way is a 14-mile trail across Stockport borough from Woodford in the south to Reddish in the north. It is named after a local man who was the last Englishman to win a singles title at Wimbledon.

3 Cross the main road and turn right and left into Robins Lane to pass Bramhall church on your right. At the mini roundabout, go ahead onto a cobbled path and through a gate to walk between a golf course and what eventually becomes a wooded ravine. Cross the road ahead onto a footpath into Bramhall Park. At the fork, bear

right to walk along the left-hand edge of a car park. Cross a drive and walk ahead to the entrance to Bramall Hall.

4 Turn left and then right by the ha-ha and take the steps down to the lake. Turn right, cross a stone bridge and take a left fork to follow the Lady Brook. Where tracks cross, turn left along the main drive. At the lodge, turn right, cross the road by the pedestrian crossing and go left and right into Bridge Lane.

5 Find the entrance to Happy Valley on your right. At a junction of paths, turn left to cross a wooden bridge. (There are stepping stones further along for the more adventurous.) Turn right to follow the brook. Go over a stile and continue alongside the brook, ignoring a farm track. Where the path turns sharply left, do not go up the steps, but bear right along a bank at the edge of a meadow to emerge onto a lane.

6 Turn right, cross the bridge and turn left to pass a red house. At a house called Coppice End, go onto a narrow path. Go through a large metal kissing gate and where the path appears to divide, bear slightly right up the bank. Go through a gate onto a narrower path, cross a bridge and a stile, and head uphill towards the road. Cross it, walk up the steps and turn left to return to the car park.

Places of interest nearby

Largely 16th-century **Bramall Hall** is well worth a visit (☎ 0161 485 3708; postcode SK7 3NX). Younger walkers, however, may prefer **Brookside Garden Centre**, where there is both a miniature and a model railway. It is only a quarter of a mile north of Anglesey Drive along the A532. ☎ 01625 872919; postcode SK12 1BY.

7 Bartington

The Holly Bush

Bartington is a tiny hamlet on the A49. From it we walk to the slightly larger but very peaceful village of Little Leigh and down into the Weaver valley. Here we see the Weaver Navigation, a river improvement authorized in 1720 so that salt could be taken from the mid-Cheshire salt mines to Merseyside for industrial and domestic use, and the Trent and Mersey Canal of 1777, which took it to Staffordshire where it was used to glaze pottery. Several of the local footpaths are blocked so this is a walk largely along quiet country lanes and none the worse for that.

Distance – 4 miles.

OS map Explorer 267 Northwich and Delamere Forest (GR: SJ606770).

Starting point The Holly Bush, Bartington. The pub car park can be used by patrons while they walk but please seek permission. Unfortunately, bends in the narrow lanes make roadside parking inadvisable.

How to get there *The Holly Bush is on the east side of the A49 Warrington–Whitchurch road, ¼ mile south of its junction with the A533 Norwich–Runcorn road and 2¼ miles north of the Weaverham bypass.*

Largely a gentle stroll along quiet lanes, though there is a little field walking and a sometimes muddy bridleway.

THE PUB

The **Holly Bush** is a pub of two parts – a timbered and thatched cottage dating from 1641 and a brick-built extension of 1848. Once a farm as well as a pub, its barn and granary now provide overnight accommodation. The menu is international and includes pork fillet in Szechuan sauce, duck medallions in a hot sweet chilli sauce, Aberdeen Angus beef lasagne, beef jalfrezi and chicken breast in Dijon mustard and black pepper sauce. There are several vegetarian meals and a children's menu. The beers served are Tetley Cask and Smooth, plus a guest beer.

Open from 12 noon to 3 pm and from 5 pm to 11 pm Monday to Saturday and from 12 noon to 11 pm Sunday. Food is served from 12 noon to 2 pm and from 5.30 pm to 9 pm Monday to Saturday and 12 noon to 9 pm on Sunday. ☎ 01606 853196; postcode CW8 4QY.

1 From the pub car park, turn right into Smithy Lane, taking care on its bends. Go ahead at the junction to pass a plant nursery and farm produce shop on your left. Cross the busy main road with care to enter the much quieter Ash House Lane. Bear right at the junction with Heath Lane. The letters on the large datestones along here stand for Northwich Rural District Council and Little Leigh Housing Association.

2 At the little Baptist chapel of 1829, turn right into Shutley Lane. Notice the strange many windowed façade of Heath Lodge to the left and the view towards Frodsham Hill to the right.

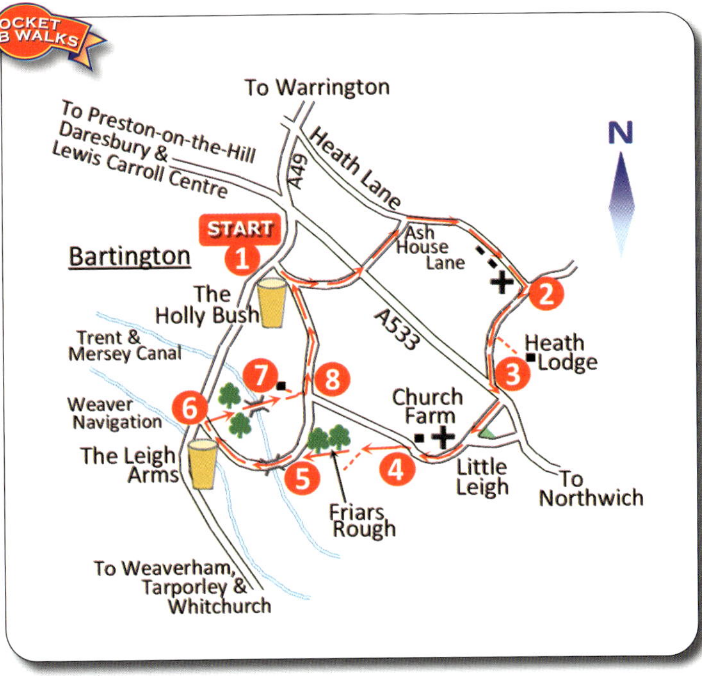

The River Weaver

3 At the main road go left and then right at the Cheshire Cycleway sign to walk into Little Leigh village. Bear right at the small green towards St Michael's church. Built in the 1870s from local handmade bricks, it replaced an earlier church on the opposite side of the road, where its lych-gate originally stood. It is usually open on Saturdays in summer, a quiz leaflet about the building being provided for children.

4 From the church bear right and, after passing Church Farm on the right, turn left into a bridleway. This can be muddy in spring but its hazards are compensated for by the views across the Weaver valley towards Delamere Forest and by the wild flowers at its side. Where the track swings left into a field, go ahead onto a narrower path alongside Friars Rough Wood.

5 At the path's end, turn left to cross the Trent and Mersey Canal. Now follow the high-hedged lane to the 280-year-old Leigh Arms, where you might like to stop for refreshment and a look at the canalized River Weaver.

6 Turn right at the pub and look for a footpath on the right alongside the drive to a house. Walk between the garden fence and a hawthorn hedge, through a gap by some roses and along the right-hand edge of a field. The path then rises through some ivy-clad trees to cross the canal. Look right here and you will see the 15th-century tower of Weaverham church.

7 Go through a kissing gate and keep along the left-hand edge of a meadow. Do not let the presence of (usually docile) cattle deter you from looking back to enjoy the excellent views. Look out for a kissing gate onto a broad, mown path. Turn right onto a farmhouse drive and walk away from the house.

8 At the drive's end, turn left into a particularly attractive lane. Enjoy its trees and wild flowers, the swifts on its telephone wires and the pleasant rural views through the gaps in its high hedges. At its end, turn left to return to the Holly Bush.

Places of interest nearby

At Daresbury, some 5 miles north-west of the Holly Bush is the **Lewis Carroll Centre**. It has displays relating to the author's life and *Alice's Adventures in Wonderland* and *Through the Looking Glass*, while the adjoining church has a window with characters from the books. Close by is the National Trust-managed **Lewis Carroll Birthplace site**. ☎ 01925 740348; postcode WA4 4AE.

8 Gawsworth

The Harrington Arms

With its elm avenues, ornamental lakes, handsome old houses and pretty 15th-century church, Gawsworth is regarded by many as Cheshire's loveliest village. From its inn we walk along an avenue said to be haunted by Mary Fitton, possibly the 'Dark Lady' of Shakespeare's sonnets. We then pass through a pleasant pastoral landscape before venturing into National Trust woodland to see the grave of Maggoty Johnson, the

Distance – 3¼ miles.

OS map Explorer 268 Wilmslow, Macclesfield and Congleton (GR: SJ887694).

Starting point The Harrington Arms, Gawsworth. The pub's car park is very small and it would be advisable to find a spot close by on Church Lane.

How to get there *The Harrington Arms lies just to the east of the A536, 4 miles north of its junction with the A34 at Congleton and 2½ miles south of its junction with the B5088 at Macclesfield.*

A pleasant stroll across gently undulating countryside and through a delightful village.

country's last household jester. Enjoying excellent views of the Pennines, we walk on to the hamlet of Moss Houses on the edge of Danes Moss. Finally, we head across the fields and along another shady avenue back to Gawsworth.

THE PUB

The **Harrington Arms** takes its name from the Earls of Harrington, former occupants of Gawsworth Hall. A 17th-century farmhouse with an 18th-century extension, it has been serving beer since 1810. A Robinson's house, its meals are freshly made from first-class local ingredients. Along with more traditional pub grub like cottage pie, sausage and mash and various steaks, there is pork chop served with black pudding hash brown in a leek, cream and cider sauce, and chicken with smoked bacon and Shropshire blue cheese. Vegetarian dishes, light bites and sandwiches are also available in this former coaching house.

Open from 12 noon to 3 pm and 5 pm to 11.30 pm on weekdays and 12 noon to 4 pm and 7 pm to 11 pm on Sundays. Food is served from 12 noon to 2.30 pm (3.30 pm on Sundays) and 5 pm to 8.30 pm.
☎ 01260 223325; postcode SK11 9JR.

1 From the Harrington Arms, walk north along Church Lane past the Georgian rectory and the steps to the church. Where the road swings to the right, turn left to a stile. Walk along the tree-shaded right bank of what was once an ornamental lake and then a well-

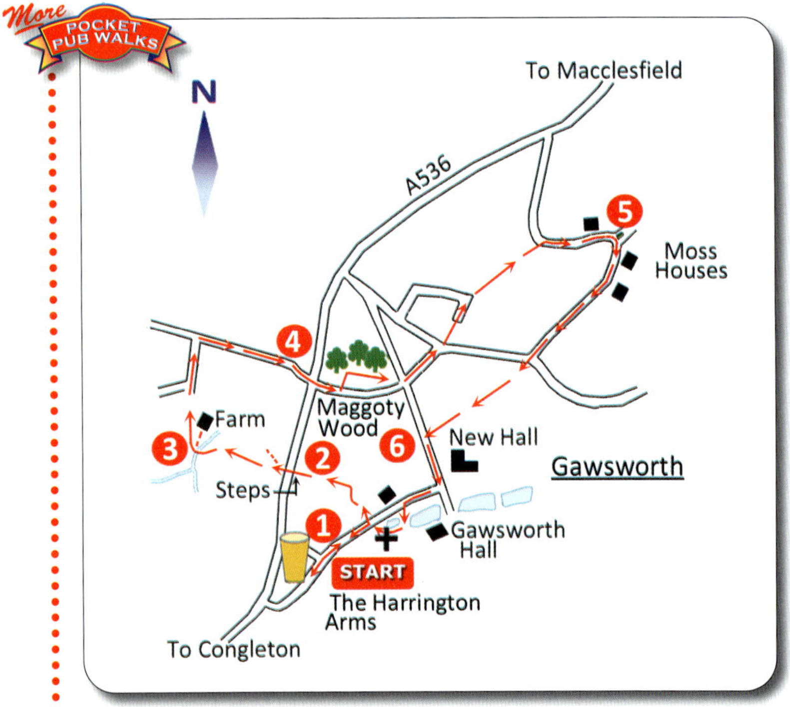

The Tudor old hall at Gawsworth

worn path through a meadow. By a makeshift sheep pen and hawthorn hedge, drop down to a stile on the left. Walk up the bank, alongside the fence and down the steps.

2 Cross the road with care and take the path ahead between two wire fences. Go through a gate and follow a just discernible path across a meadow to a kissing gate. Continue across some more open pasture and bear left to follow a stream to another metal gate.

3 Turn right. Do not go up the bank to the farm, but pass through a large metal gate to walk between a meadow and the farmhouse garden. Go down the drive with its damson and crab apple trees, carry on ahead along a sunken metalled lane and turn right at the T-junction.

4 Cross the main road into Maggoty Lane. Ignore the first track on the left and enter Maggoty Wood at the National Trust sign. Walk up the bank past the bluebell conservation area and turn right at the top to pass Maggoty Johnson's grave on your left. Go through the kissing gate and ahead into Wardle Crescent, which oddly is not a crescent but a lane. At the T-junction, go ahead onto a narrow footpath between the houses. Emerging onto a cul-de-sac, walk on past a large beech tree onto another path. Cross a stile and walk along the right-hand edge of a field to cross another stile onto a short wooded track. On meeting a lane, continue ahead to Moss Houses.

5 At the triangular green, turn right and, noting how many houses have the word 'moss' in their names, walk on to a T-junction. Go over the stile ahead and across a small field to a stile and gate into a larger meadow. Walk alongside the fence to your left and cross a stile onto a lane.

6 Turn left and walk past the handsome 18th-century New Hall. If you wish to visit Tudor Gawsworth Hall, carry on ahead; otherwise follow the road round to the right and enjoy the views of it across the lake. At the lake's end, turn left to visit the church. It is usually open and is well worth seeing. From the churchyard, you can catch a glimpse of the medieval Old Rectory across the road. Now descend the steps and return to the Harrington Arms.

Place of interest nearby

Gawsworth Hall is a must both for the house itself and for its beautiful gardens, which host open-air theatre, concerts and craft fairs. ☎ 01260 223456; postcode SK11 9RN.

9 Hatchmere

The Carriers Inn

Hatchmere, the hamlet, is named after Hatch Mere, the lake in Delamere Forest. The forest is a relic of a medieval hunting forest whose deciduous trees have been augmented by conifers planted by the Forestry Commission. Its meres, some of which are now peat mosses, started life as kettle holes – hollows left by retreating glaciers. Younger walkers will probably be more interested in the Hebridean sheep and donkeys we see as we walk from our pub and alongside Flaxmere to

Distance – 6 miles, with the option of an extra mile.

OS map Explorer 267 Northwich & Delamere Forest (GR: SJ556721).

Starting point The Carriers Inn, Hatchmere. Customers may leave their cars in the pub car park whilst they walk, but please ask the manager's permission. Alternately, use the Forestry Commission car park, close to Delamere station and start the walk at point 5 (GR: SJ555704).

How to get there *The Carriers Inn is on the B5152 Tarporley-Frodsham road, about 2½ miles north of its junction with the A556 from Manchester to Chester.*

Apart from the optional last mile, which can be muddy after rain, this is a pleasant easy walk with just a few slight inclines.

peaceful Norley. Its noble church was designed by the architect of Truro cathedral. From Norley, we walk through a particularly attractive stretch of forest and close by the waters of Dead Lake before skirting the shores of Blakemere. Those with the courage and energy then have the option of doing an almost complete circuit of Hatch Mere before finding rest and refreshment in the Carriers Inn.

The **Carriers Inn** dates from 1637 and incorporates the former village smithy. Today it is a smart pub/restaurant with views over the mere from its rear windows. It prides itself on only serving food made from the freshest of ingredients and all the puddings are home-made. In addition to pub stalwarts like fish and chips and the Sunday roast, the dishes on offer include chicken satay, salmon in crayfish sauce, roasted Gressingham duck and fillet of venison. Omelettes and other lighter meals are available, as are vegetarian dishes. Beers include Marston's Burton Bitter and Wychwood Brewery's Hobgoblin.

Open from 11 am to 11 pm every day. Food is served from 11 am to 9.30 pm. ☎ 01928 787877; postcode WA6 6NL.

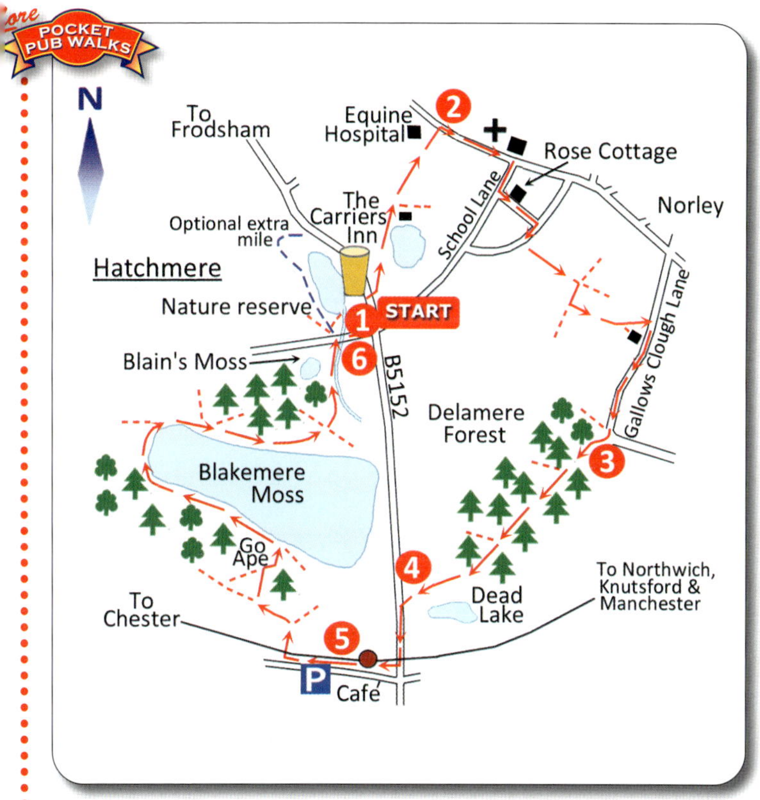

1 From the pub, cross the road and walk up a track. Follow it round to the left, passing Flaxmere in the trees to your right. On reaching a house, go ahead onto a narrow track between fields. Go through the hedge to the right of a gate and walk alongside the paddocks of an equine hospital.

2 Turn right to pass Norley church, right again into School Lane and left by Rose Cottage and Mill Cottage. At the T-junction, turn right and take the bridleway on the left. After walking a narrow path between hedges, go through a gate and along the right bank of a dry valley. Cross a stile and turn right. Ignore the first track on the left and go up a sunken lane. Turn left at the sign for Gallowsclough Lane. On reaching some houses, bear left and turn right into the lane.

3 At the sharp bend, turn right onto a bridleway. Keep left at a junction of paths and continue along a sunken lane. Go through a gap in a fence to enter Delamere Forest. Keep along the main track, initially following the Delamere Way signs. At the point where the track swings sharply right, go straight ahead up the rise to pass a meadow with a Dutch barn and then, in the trees, the mysterious waters of Dead Lake.

The Delamere Way is a 21½-mile walk from Frodsham to Warrington along footpaths and quiet roads.

4 Turn left onto the road, cross the railway bridge, take the steps on the right and perhaps call at the Station House Café for some Cheshire Farm ice cream.

5 Walk to the far end of the adjacent Forestry Commission car park and take the path on the right past the picnic tables. At its end, turn right and cross the railway bridge. Pass through the barrier ahead and turn right at the Linmere Trail sign.

Delamere Forest

The Linmere Trail (1¾ miles) is one of three marked walking routes through the forest. The others are the Blakemere Trail (2¾ miles) and the Easi Trail (¾ mile).

Follow the main path round to the right at the first junction, to pass part of the Go Ape assault course on your left. At the cross-path, turn left onto a wide track. Go over another cross-path and turn right at a T-junction. At a cross-track by a picnic table, follow the sign for Whitemoor Gates. At the junction, do not go up the hill but bear right. Ignore the path on the left and continue past the bench along the north bank of Blakemere. As you near the road, go across the junction onto a narrower path and follow a stream. Approaching a house, follow the path away from the stream and have a look at Blain's Moss, to your left, before you descend to the road.

6 Here the adventurous walker has the opportunity to walk around Hatch Mere by crossing the road and entering the nature reserve. If you do, take the second track off the main path, head across the moss towards a white post and then turn right to eventually reach the Carriers Inn. The less adventurous should turn right into the road and then left to return to the pub.

Place of interest nearby

Abbeywood is a 45-acre estate surrounding an Edwardian house. It has a rose-tree arboretum and several themed gardens, while its orangery, vegetable garden and greenhouse grow food for its café. There is an entrance fee but no charge for children. It is 2¾ miles south of Hatchmere and reached shortly after turning right off the B5152 onto the A556. ☎ 01606 889477; postcode CW8 2HW.

More POCKET PUB WALKS

10 Christleton

The Cheshire Cat

Christleton and neighbouring Waverton are villages on the Duke of Westminster's Cheshire estate. You can see his crest of a Talbot dog on the farmhouse gateposts and it is said that the medieval towers of the churches were given their little spires to aid the first Duke in his favourite sport of steeple-chasing. We walk along the towpath of the Shropshire Union Canal, authorised in 1793 to link the Severn with the Dee, from our pub into Christleton village. Amongst its picturesque old houses are the almhouses by The Pit. We then cross farmland to the historic heart of Waverton before picking up the canal again.

Distance – 6½ or 6 miles.

OS map Explorer 266 Wirral and Chester (GR SJ441651).

Starting point The Cheshire Cat at Christleton. Patrons may leave their cars in the car park while they walk, but please seek permission. Otherwise, use the public car park in Eggbridge Lane, 1¼ miles south, and start the walk from there.

How to get there *The Cheshire Cat is just off the A41 Whitchurch-Chester road 7½ miles north of its junction with the A534 and ½ mile south of the A55 flyover.*

A largely level walk down quiet lanes, across fields and along a canal towpath.

The **Cheshire Cat**, originally a manor house, was a wartime intelligence centre and a chicken farm before it became a pub. With fourteen bedrooms, it is the ideal base for a walking holiday on the Welsh border. As well as various sandwiches and wraps, there are daily specials which generally include two vegetarian dishes. Amongst the tempting main courses are sole and smoked salmon roulade, Scottish venison, Shropshire chicken and duck leg confit. Desserts include raspberry crème brûlée, scrumpy poached pear and sticky toffee, date and ginger pudding. Thwaites' ales are on draught and there is usually at least one guest beer.

Open from 11 am to 11 pm. Food is served from 12 noon to 10 pm Monday to Saturday and 12 noon till 9.30 pm Sunday. ☎ 01244 332200; postcode CH3 6AE.

1 From the Cheshire Cat's garden, turn left onto the canal towpath. Go under a bridge, turn left and cross it. At the lane, go left again, then right into Christleton village. Turn left at the village pump and right at The Pit, once a clay pit, now a delightful small lake. But for the voracious ducks, this would be an excellent spot for a picnic.

2 Approaching a children's playground, turn into a track to your right. Cross a stile and keep along the right-hand edge of the field. Pass through a gap in a hedge and turn left. Follow the path as it swings right and go left at the junction. By the clay pit, cross a stile and go right and immediately left to another. Bear slightly right across the field, leave it by a stile and turn left onto a lane.

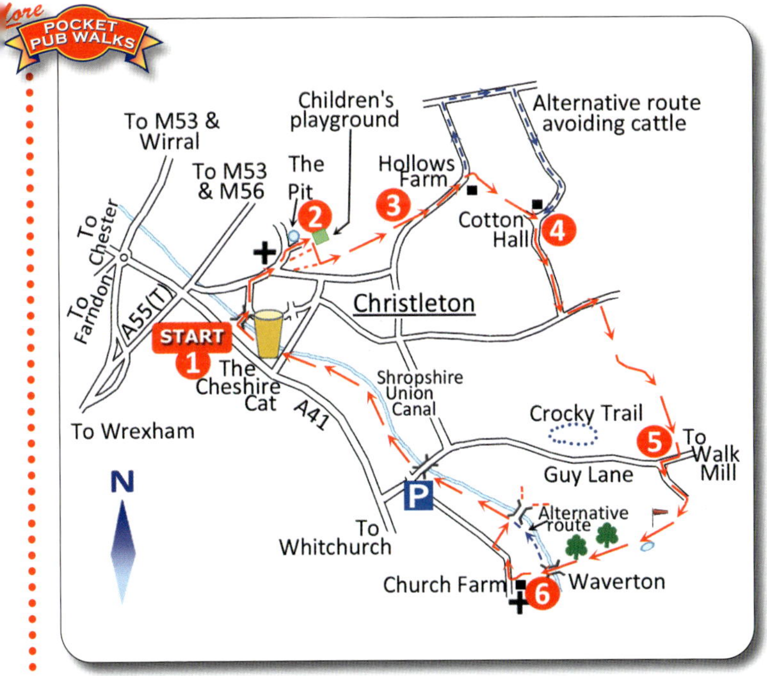

Church Farm, seen at point 6 of the walk

3 Walk along the lane with its views of Helsby and Eddisbury hills until you have passed Hollows Farm. Cross the stile on the right and walk along the right-hand edge of the field. (There may be cows in this field. If this worries you, stay on the lane and turn right and right again to get to point 4.) After a plank bridge and stile, go up an incline and cross another bridge in the hedge. Follow a well-defined path through the crop and head to the right of the farm buildings. Walk to the road junction by Cotton Hall.

4 Turn right onto the lane and left at the T-junction. Ignore the first opening on the right and take the one by the footpath sign. Go along the left-hand edge of the field, cross two sets of bridges and stiles, and turn left to a third. Now head to the right of Peckforton

and Beeston castles on their respective hills but, if no path has been left through the crop, stay on the field's left-hand edge. Cross a bridge under a large oak. Take the path ahead to another bridge and walk alongside a stream to a gap by a broken stile.

5 Go right and left into Martins Lane. After the farm entrance, turn right into a field and head towards the left of a flying club's windsock. Go through a gap in a hedge and pass a pond on your left. Keep ahead at the next gap, with a wood, Waverton Gorse, to your right. Walk to the left of a gate and look for a path on the right, just before the top of the field. Bear left and go over the canal bridge.

6 Here you may join the towpath and return to the car, saving ½ mile. If, however, you wish to experience the delights of Waverton, carry on between the high hedges to emerge in the village by the imposing Church Farm. Here turn right and then right again at a footpath sign. Walk a short track, go through a kissing gate and then through another on the right. Turn left and walk along the edge of a park-like field. After another kissing gate, go down some steps and turn left onto the towpath to pass the Eggbridge Lane car park and return to the Cheshire Cat.

Places of interest nearby

If younger walkers have any energy left, they may wish to use it up on the **Crocky Trail**, a junior assault course incorporating the madcap inventions of a local agricultural engineer. It is signposted off the A41, just over a mile south of the Cheshire Cat. ☎ 01244 336161; postcode CH3 7PH.

For something more sedate, go a little further along to the **Walk Mill**, where you can watch the corn being ground as you eat cakes made from the mill's own flour. ☎ 01829 749373; postcode CH3 7RZ.

11 Little Budworth

The Red Lion

Little Budworth, with its sandstone church, almhouses, thatched and timbered cottages and red telephone box seems at first sight to be an old-fashioned country village. It is something of a shock to come across a 'suburban' housing estate soon after the start of the walk. This, however, is soon forgotten as we cross the fields towards Darley Hall and the moat of its medieval predecessor. From then on, the walk is a delightful stroll along a stream-edged lane rich in trees and wild flowers. This is best enjoyed on weekdays, as at weekends its birdsong can be drowned out by the sound of cars racing round the adjacent Oulton Park track.

Distance – 2¾ miles.

OS map Explorer 267 Northwich and Delamere Forest (GR: SJ598653).

Starting point The Red Lion, Little Budworth. Patrons may use the pub car park while they walk but should seek permission. Alternatively, it should be possible to find a parking spot round the corner in St Peter's Drive without inconveniencing the residents.

How to get there *The pub is in Vicarage Lane, Little Budworth, and can be reached by turning south-east off the A49 Warrington–Whitchurch road, ½ mile south of its junction with the A54 Winsford–Chester road.*

A pleasant stroll which can be enjoyed by all ages.

THE PUB

The Red Lion is a traditional village inn with a welcoming open fire. A Robinson's house, it uses the brewery's Unicorn bitter in its excellent steak and ale pie. Other dishes on its extensive menu include a curry of the day, fresh salmon in a tomato Provençal sauce, cherry tomato and mushroom risotto and toasted pepper and goat's cheese salad. There is a traditional Sunday lunch, while an afternoon tea of sandwiches, scones and dessert is available from Monday to Saturday.

Open from 12 noon to 11 pm. Food is served all day. ☎ *01829 760275; postcode CW6 9BY.*

1 Turn left out of the Red Lion's car park and right into St Peter's Drive. Pass Yew Tree Close on the left and turn left at the T-junction.

At the end of the cul-de-sac, look for a footpath sign on the left and pass between the gardens of two houses. Turn right and walk between a garden and a barbed wire fence, watching out for brambles and nettles.

2 Cross a stile and go ahead across a field to another stile. Walk past a solitary oak and a cattle trough to a footbridge and stile. With some mixed deciduous and coniferous woodland to your right, continue ahead to another bridge and stile. Beyond a stand of trees on a slight rise, follow a path through the crops, heading between farm buildings on the left and cottages on the right. Cross a stile (looking out for a possible electric fence) and then a bridge over a brook, and head towards the tall trees just to the right of the farm. Pass Darley Hall's moat on your left and cross a stile.

3 After looking back for a moment to enjoy the view of the pastoral landscape you have passed through, walk along the drive away

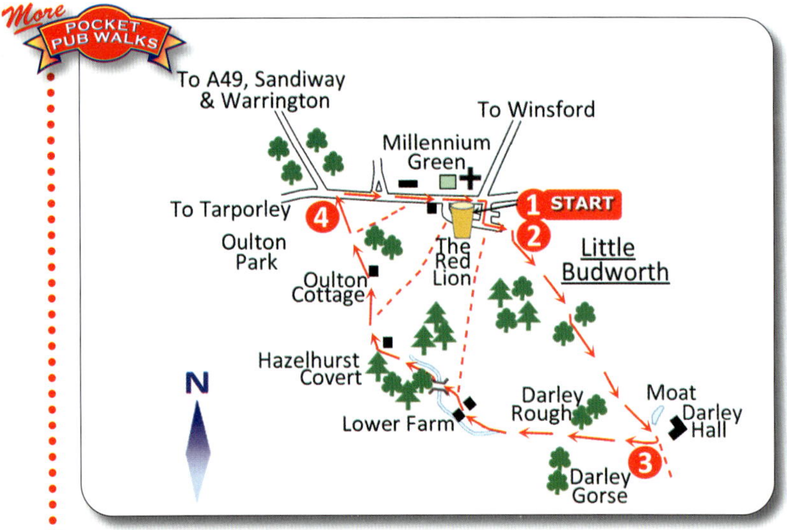

from the hall with the oak, sycamore and birch woodland of Darley Rough immediately to your right and Darley Gorse across the field to your left.

Where the landscape becomes more open, look for celadine growing on the bank of the stream to your right. It is worth pausing to enjoy the scene around Lower Farm, with its beeches and copper beeches, and ducks on the stream where it flows through its garden.

After a shaded section with wood anemones beneath the elms, there are open views towards a stand of pines, while Hazelhurst Covert to the left of the lane is something of an arboretum, with its interesting mix of conifers and deciduous trees. If you stop for a moment, you may hear the songs of greenfinch and chiffchaff. Beyond a stable block on the right there are good views towards the medieval tower of Little Budworth church. To your left is the walled garden of Oulton Park, whose mansion was demolished after a fire in 1926. Then, after Oulton Cottage, with its weeping willow, there is a plantation of young trees, including the comparatively rare sweet chestnut.

4 At the end of the lane, with its rebuilt section of park wall, turn right into Little Budworth. Notice the almhouses of 1734 on the left and the thatched and diminutive Old Vicarage on the right. Then pass the Millennium Green and play area and return to the Red Lion.

Place of interest nearby

Cheshire Falconry, 4¾ miles north of Little Budworth, is a bird of prey centre with owls, eagles, falcons and hawks. The falconry is adjacent to Blakemere Craft and Garden Centre, near Sandiway. It is reached by turning right off the A49 onto the A556 Chester–Northwich road. ☎ 01606 882223; postcode CW8 2EB.

12 Darnhall

The Old Star

Darnhall is a hamlet in the parish of Over. The latter place was a medieval market town but is now part of Winsford, home to Cheshire's only remaining salt mine. As a result of mining subsidence, two lakes or flashes have been formed in the valley of the River Weaver. The larger Bottom Flash is now something of a resort with fishing and boating. Our walk takes us along a lovely lime avenue to Over's 16th-century church and through a farmyard to Bottom Flash. We then return to the Old Star, by way of farmland and woodland. The pub has a horse on

Distance – 3½ miles.

OS map Explorer 267 Northwich and Delamere Forest (GR: SJ647650).

Starting point The Old Star, Darnhall. Park, with permission, in the pub car park or over the way on Darnhall School Lane.

How to get there *The Old Star is on the B5074 Winsford–Nantwich road, ¾ mile south of its junction with the A54 and 8 miles north of Nantwich town centre.*

Apart from three fairly steep banks, this is level, easy walking. There are plenty of stiles but these are due to be replaced by kissing gates.

its sign and you are likely to see horses, sheep and even Highland cattle on this very pleasant stroll.

The **Old Star**, which once doubled as a farmhouse, has been in existence since at least the 1780s. It serves Black Sheep bitter, as well as Cheshire-brewed ales from the Northern Brewery in Sandiway. The food available is simple but wholesome pub grub such as home-made soup, an all-day breakfast, gammon with egg or pineapple, fish and chips and a pie of the day. There are hot and cold sandwiches to eat in or take away and fillings include egg mayonnaise, ham and tomato, steak and cheese, and brie, cranberry and bacon.

Open 12 noon to 12 midnight Monday to Saturday, 12 noon to 11 pm Sunday. Food is served from 7.30 am to 3 pm Monday to Friday and from 7.30 am to 1 pm on Saturday. No food is available in the evening or on Sundays. ☎ 01606 556557; postcode CW7 4BL.

1 From the pub, turn right and right again into the avenue. As you approach the church and a replica of the fire-damaged, medieval Blue Bell Inn, bear left and go along a track marked 'For Access Only'. Pass Church Hill farmhouse and go through the farmyard onto a farm track. Do not follow the track where it begins to go downhill into a dry valley, but bear left to walk along the left-hand edge of the field.

2 Pass through a kissing gate and turn right onto a stony lane. At the junction by the Lakeside Caravan Park, turn right again. Enjoy the lovely views of Bottom Flash through the gaps in the hedge to your left.

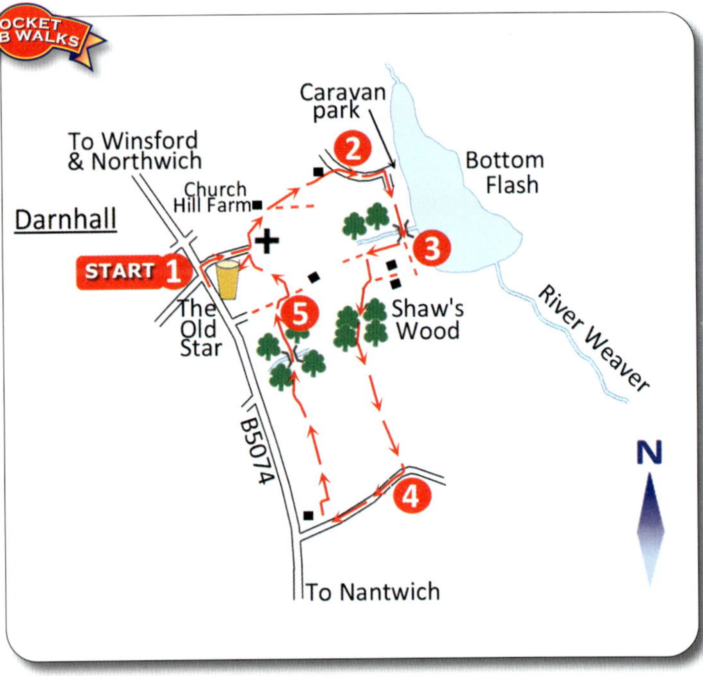

Bottom Flash marina

3 After passing a wooded ravine on your right, turn right to a stile. Climb the bank to another stile and bear right to follow the edge of the wood. After the next stile, turn left to walk along the left-hand edge of a field. On reaching a concrete road, turn right onto a track and follow it round to the left. Pass through a metal gate into Shaw's Wood. Coming into the open, cross a stile and walk to the far right-hand corner of the meadow. Go into the next meadow and walk along its right-hand edge. Pass through a gap in the hedge ahead and continue forward to a metal gate.

4 Turn right onto a concrete lane. Pass a farm on your left and turn right at a public footpath sign. Cross a stile and walk diagonally right across the paddock to a wooden gate. Remembering to close the gate behind you, go along the right-hand edge of the next paddock and through a metal gate. Walk along the left-hand side

of a big field with long views to the right. Cross a plank bridge and stile, and walk ahead to a kissing gate beneath an ash tree. Now bear slightly left to another kissing gate, cross a farm road and pass through a further gate. Cross the field to a stile and plank bridge almost directly ahead in a hawthorn hedge. Go diagonally right to cross a ladder stile and then bear left to another stile. This will take you into woodland. Go down the steps to a footbridge and up the bank to a stile. Keep to the left-hand edge of the field to pass through a gap in a hedge. There are likely to be cattle here. Continue ahead and skirt the field until you come to a stile in a corner.

5 Turn right onto a farm track. As you approach the farmhouse, cross a stile on your left. Go along the left-hand edge of a field, with good views of Winsford to the right. Turn left and go through a gate to walk alongside the churchyard fence. Cross the stile and turn left. Where the avenue begins, take a path on the left which ends by the Old Star car park.

Place of interest nearby

Weaver Hall, Northwich, 7 miles north of Over via the A54, A5018 and A533, is the museum of Cheshire's salt industry. Some of its displays also relate to the building's former life as a workhouse and there is a quiz to help children explore its galleries. ☎ 01606 271640; postcode CW9 8AB.

More POCKET PUB WALKS

13 Haslington

The Hawk Inn

Haslington, with its 16th- and 17th-century houses and cottages, is the starting point of this delightful walk. It takes us first to Haslington Hall, a splendid example of a Cheshire timbered country house. Little known now, between the wars it was well-known for its social gatherings, Agatha Christie being a frequent guest. We reach it along Park Road, through fields which were once the hall's deer park. Then we walk along an idyllic country lane to pass a farm. Finally, we cross a golf course and head back to the village over Slaughter Hill, the scene of a skirmish in the Civil War, when Haslington was pillaged by Royalist soldiers.

Distance – 3 miles.

OS map Explorer 257 Crewe & Nantwich (GR: SJ738559).

Starting point The Hawk Inn, Haslington. The pub car park is available for customers while walking but do ask permission. Otherwise, use the public car park in Waterloo Road, a short distance to the south.

How to get there *Haslington is approximately 1 mile east of the junction of the A534 with the A532, on the outskirts of Crewe and 4½ miles via the A534 from junction 17 on the M6.*

A delightful stroll along level ground with just one brief uphill stretch towards the end.

The **Hawk Inn** is over 500 years old and the wattle and daub exposed on its inside walls testify to the fact. Reputed to have had Dick Turpin as a guest, it is a completely unspoiled place of cosy little rooms serving Robinson's ale brewed to an 1890s' recipe. Its home-cooked food is straightforward but excellent and includes steaks, chops, liver and bacon, and various omelettes.

Open from 12 noon to 12 midnight. Food is served from 12 noon to 2 pm. ☎ 01270 582181; postcode CW1 5RG

1 Turn right out of the pub car park and left by a timbered and thatched cottage. You are now on Park Road. Go over a cattle grid and, ignoring a footpath sign on the right, cross another.

2 At the gate to Haslington Hall, with its confusing set of signs, go straight ahead until you are level with the house. Turn left and go down the drive, passing a pond on your right. Turn right onto a lane and, after passing Heathfield Farm, turn right again.

3 Go down the farm lane towards Hall o' the Heath's donkey paddock. Before reaching the farm's outbuildings, leave the main track and bear right and left to a kissing gate. Pass through the wooden gate ahead, continue through a kissing gate and walk along the right-hand edge of the field to another. Continue along the right-hand edge of the next field, cross a stile and continue ahead. Go through a kissing gate and cross a flagged path. Walk ahead through the rough of a golf course, passing to the right of a pond. Continue ahead and walk beneath the trees to pass the mower shed and club house.

4 At the end of the car park, look on the left for a marker post onto a narrow path. Cross a stile and continue ahead across sheep pasture past a broken stile. Go over the next stile onto a narrow footpath with the impressive Amicia Tenement, once the home of

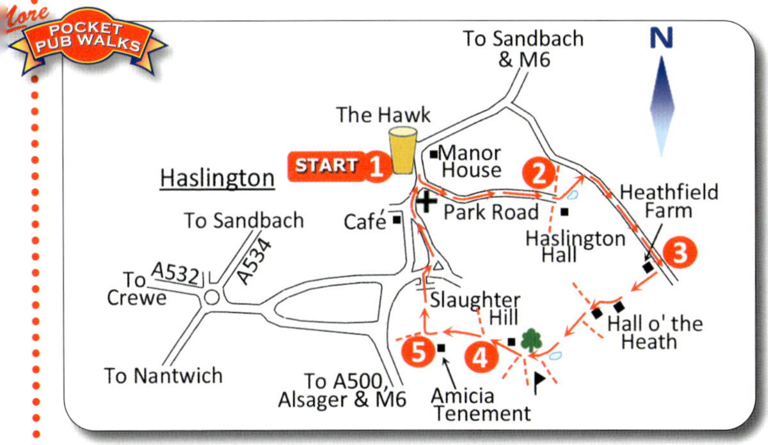

Delightful 16th-century cottages on the route

Lord Crewe, on the left. Go through a kissing gate and continue ahead along the right-hand edge of a meadow to another.

5 Turn sharp right to climb Slaughter Hill. Keep along the right-hand edge of the field, go through a kissing gate and follow a narrow path between fields to a stile. Go ahead along an unmade road to a T-junction. Turn right, then go left into Cross Road and ahead into Waterloo Road. At its end, turn right to pass Haslington's pretty, little Georgian church on your way back to the Hawk Inn.

Place of interest nearby

Crewe Heritage Centre, Vernon Way, Crewe, is largely concerned with Crewe's history as a major railway junction and locomotive manufacturing town. There is an exhibition hall, miniature and model railways, and occasional visits from steam locomotives. ☎ 01270 212130; postcode CW1 2DB.

14 Shocklach

The Bull

Shocklach is now an exceptionally peaceful place but, thanks to its situation close to the Welsh border, it has had a turbulent past. In fact, although this walk starts with a visit to a rare breeds farm, it is really one for history buffs. It takes us to a Norman church and the site of a border castle, along an ancient drove road and across the ridges and furrows made by medieval ploughs. Our outward journey is on the Marches Way and has views west towards the Clwydian Hills of North Wales. We return along the Bishop Bennet Way, and to our left can be seen Bickerton Hill, with its Iron Age hill-fort.

Distance – 4¾ miles.

OS map Explorer 257 Crewe & Nantwich (GR: SJ439492).

Starting point The Bull Inn, Shocklach. With permission, use the pub car park. Roadside parking is difficult on Shocklach's narrow lanes.

How to get there *The Bull is on the unclassified Farndon–Worthenbury road, 3¼ miles south of its junction with the A534 and B5130 at Farndon, and 2 miles north of its junction with the B5069 near Threapwood.*

Generally easy walking across fields and along country lanes, though there are lots of stiles.

The **Bull** is a welcoming village inn whose owners pride themselves on providing enjoyable food made from local produce. Meals range from light bites like baked Cheshire brie studded with rosemary and garlic and black pudding and smoked bacon hash cake to the traditional Sunday joint which, if pre-ordered, will be brought to your table for you to carve. As well as the usual pub grub such as steak pie and chips, and sausage and mash, there are also seafood, meaty and vegetarian sharing platters, while 'Little Tums' have their own menu. A free house, the Bull usually offers a choice of three draught beers.

Open from 12 noon to 11 pm Monday to Thursday, 12 noon to 12 midnight Friday and Saturday, and 12 noon to 10.30 pm Sunday. Food is served from 12 noon to 2.30 pm and 5.30 pm to 9.30 pm Monday to Friday, and 12 noon to 9.30 pm Saturday and Sunday.
☎ *01829 250239; postcode SY14 7BL.*

1 Leave the car park by the gate to the right of the pub and cross the road into Green Lane, passing the Old Post Office on your left. At a footpath sign on the right, cross a stile and walk to the left of two prominent oaks. Cross a stile and plank bridge and walk past enclosures with unusual breeds of sheep and goats to a stile in the left-hand corner of the meadow. Follow the Marches Way signs over a series of stiles and plank bridges until you emerge onto a lane.

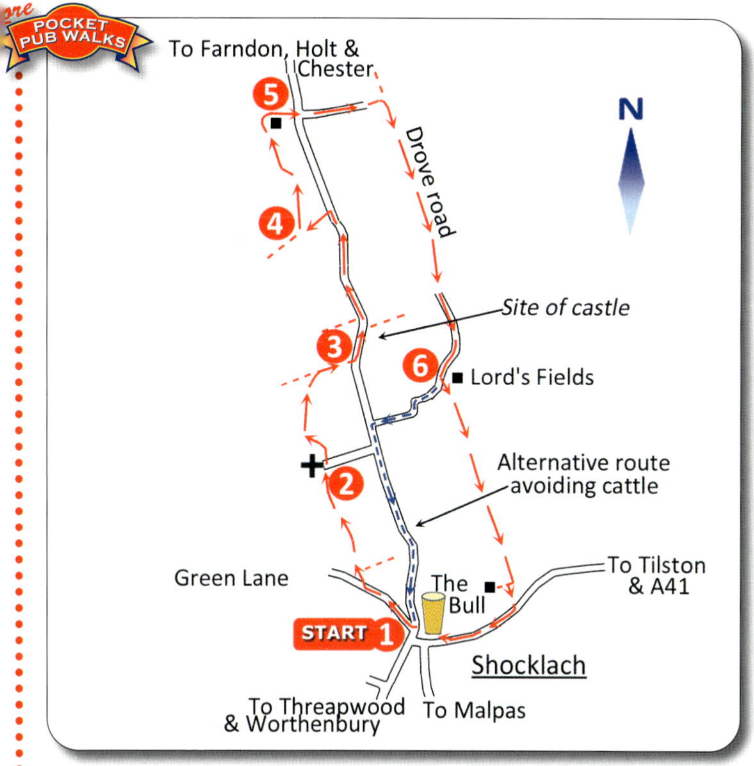

The Marches Way is a 204-mile route along the Welsh border, linking the Roman forts at Caerleon and Chester.

2 Walk ahead past the car park to the tiny Norman church of St Edith. If you do not wish to visit the church, carry on past its gate and follow the lane round to the left to cross a plank bridge and stile on the right. Go slightly to the left to cross another bridge and stile. Keep an ancient hedgerow on your left and walk to a stile in a neatly cut hedge. Here you should, in theory, walk half left into the field and turn right at a junction of paths. However, if there is a crop in the field, you should turn right and walk along its edge until you reach a gate and stile.

3 Turn left into the road. Take care. There is relatively little traffic but what there is tends to be fast-moving.

The trees on the left hide the motte of Shocklach Castle. The earthworks of its moat and bailey can be seen on the right by the drive to Castletown Farm.

Carry on along the road and take the second track on the left, which is cobbled.

4 Cross a stile on the right and walk along the left-hand edge of the field to a yellow footpath sign. Turn left and immediately right and head towards the left-hand corner of the farm buildings. Go through a gate by a redundant stile and turn right to another gate and stile. Bear right to a track between buildings and pass through two gates.

5 Cross the road onto the lane ahead and turn right at the Bishop Bennet Way sign.

The Bishop Bennet Way is a 34-mile route for riders and walkers from near Beeston Castle to Wirswall on the Shropshire border. It is named after an 18th-century Irish bishop who rode the lanes, carrying out a survey of the Roman road from Chester to Whitchurch.

This section of the walk is along a track which some believe to be a Roman road but is more likely to have been a medieval drove road. At its end, go ahead along a metalled lane until you have passed a house on the left called Lord's Fields.

6 You are now in cattle country. If you are uneasy around cows, follow the road round to the left to return to the Bull. Otherwise go through a gate on the left and cross the meadow to another gate. Turn right to walk along the edge of a field with the undulations left by medieval ploughing. Cross a stile and go across the field to a narrower part on the left. Follow the path to a stile and walk under the oaks to another by a pond. Carry on past a single oak to a further stile and follow the farm track. Beyond the fence, turn left to a stile and then right along a mown avenue. Cross a stile on the right and turn left to walk down the farm drive. At its end, turn right to return to the pub.

Place of interest nearby

The excellent **Bellis Brothers' Garden Centre** at Holt can be reached via Farndon and its medieval bridge over the Dee. They have been growing strawberries there since 1860. You can pick your own or enjoy the wonderful view of the Welsh hills from the centre's café. ☎ 01829 270304; postcode LL13 9YU.

15 Wrenbury

The Cotton Arms

Wrenbury and Marbury are two of Cheshire's loveliest villages. Both have late-medieval churches, timber-framed cottages and village greens. They are linked by the Llangollen branch of the Shropshire Union Canal and, after having a look at Wrenbury, we walk along its towpath past the curious drawbridges designed by its engineer, Thomas Telford. After a visit to Marbury and its two meres, we return to Wrenbury across fields and along a quiet lane. It is a lovely walk and a short cut is provided for the less robust rambler which turns our walk into a gentle stroll.

Distance – 6 or 3 miles.

OS map Explorer 257 Crewe & Nantwich (GR: SJ591479).

Starting point The Cotton Arms, Wrenbury. Use the pub car park with the landlord's permission or the parking bay across the road.

How to get there *Wrenbury is 6 miles south-west of the A534 in Nantwich and 3¼ miles south-east of the A49 at Cholmondeley. The Cotton Arms is in Nantwich Road.*

A largely level walk along a towpath and across fields. Crops could present problems, but an easier alternative route is provided.

The **Cotton Arms** is a 16th-century village inn. It is unusual in having been built from ships' timbers and in having a tributary of the River Weaver flowing through its cellar. What makes it really special, however, is that on Wednesday and Saturday lunchtimes and Wednesday evenings it serves a two-course gourmet meal for just £5. Booking is therefore a good idea. At other times, the dishes on offer include slow-roasted Welsh lamb, Welsh Black sirloin steak, game pie and Lancashire ballontine, i.e. chicken stuffed with black pudding and wrapped in leek, and there is always a vegetarian dish. Sandwiches, in which Cheshire cheese features prominently, are available too. The three cask ales on offer change regularly.

Open from 12 noon to 12 midnight every day. Food is served from 12 noon to 9 pm. ☎ 01270 780377; postcode CW5 8HG.

1 From the Cotton Arms, turn left and walk up the lane to the green. Turn left into Wrenbury churchyard and leave it by a kissing gate. Go ahead to a stile and another kissing gate and turn left onto the towpath. Cross the road, pass a former watermill, now a pub, on the left and cross over the infant River Weaver. On reaching Bridge 22 you have the opportunity to shorten the walk by crossing the bridge to point 6. Otherwise, continue to a bridge just before some locks and turn left onto a lane.

2 Ignore the difficult stile at the roadside and go through the next gate. Follow the track, cross a stile and follow a line of oaks. At the top of the field, turn right and cross a stile on your left. Head towards a distant obelisk. It commemorates Stapleton Cotton, Viscount Combermere, a local hero of the Napoleonic Wars. At the

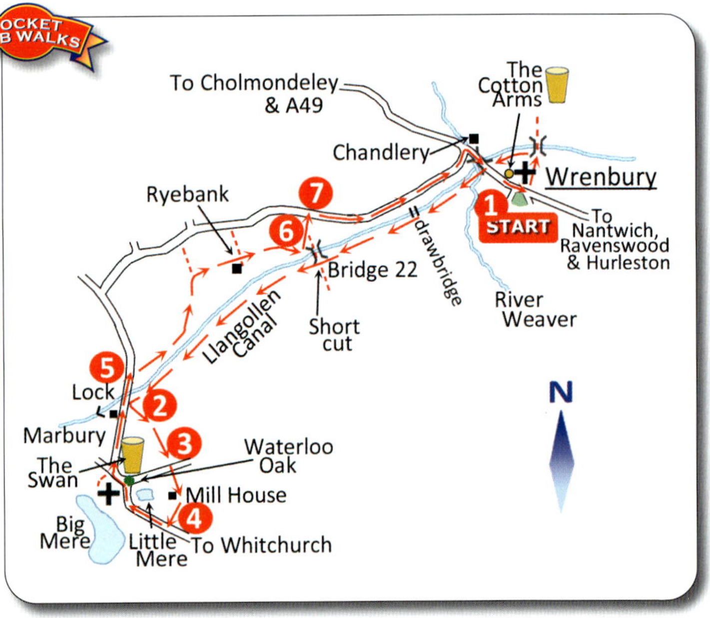

A drawbridge at Wrenbury

field's end, turn right, cross the stile and follow the hedge left to a kissing gate.

3 Cross the lane to another gate and follow the hedge on the right through dairy pasture. Do not be alarmed by the sound of barking. Labrador puppies are bred at Mill House, through the next gate, and they are safely caged. Go down the drive and turn right onto a lane.

4 The tree-shrouded Little Mere is to your right, and over the hedge to your left is Big Mere, a picturesque setting for Marbury church. Head towards the village green with its oak planted to celebrate the victory at Waterloo in 1815. Pass the Swan pub on your right and turn right into School Lane.

5 Cross the canal bridge, then a stile on the right and walk alongside the canal to cross two further stiles. Go diagonally left across a field to a gate with an arrow on its post and over a big field to a stile in a hawthorn hedge. Although the arrow here indicates a leftward direction, go diagonally right across the meadow to a stile and plank bridge. Keep along the left-hand edge of the next field, cross a stile and head towards the nearer of two farmhouses, Ryebank. Cross the farm track and walk past a trough to cross a stile. Walk along the left-hand edge of the field and cross a ramshackle bridge on your left. The official path is over the field but if there is a crop, bear right along its edge towards the canal bridge.

6 Strangely, the public footpath does not take us over the stile ahead and left along the farm track. It stays inside the fence to join the track further up via a metal gate.

7 Turn right to follow a quiet and pleasant lane past cottage gardens and a donkey paddock. At the junction, turn right to pass an old corn mill, now a chandlery, and cross a drawbridge back to the Cotton Arms.

Place of interest nearby

Snugbury's is one of several Cheshire farms making their own ice-cream. Visitors can buy the ice-cream and, by prior arrangement, tour the farm, which is on the A51(T) at Hurleston, 6 miles from Wrenbury. It can be reached by turning left off the Nantwich road for the A534 at the Ravensmoor crossroads. ☎ 01270 624830; postcode CW5 6BU.